You Can't Walk in What You Believe Until You Change the Way You Think

MICHAEL TRUSS

WESTBOW°
PRESS
A DIVISION OF THOMAS NELSON
& ZONDERVAN

Scripture taken from the King James Version of the Bible.

All Scripture quotations in this publications are from The Message.
Copyright © by Eugene H. Peterson 1993, 1994, 1995, 1996, 2000,
2001, 2002. Used by permission of NavPress Publishing Group.

WestBow Press books may be ordered through booksellers or by contacting:

WestBow Press
A Division of Thomas Nelson & Zondervan
1663 Liberty Drive
Bloomington, IN 47403
www.westbowpress.com
1 (866) 928-1240

ISBN: 978-1-4908-9240-5 (sc)
ISBN: 978-1-5127-0822-6 (e)

Print information available on the last page.

WestBow Press rev. date: 08/06/2015

CONTENTS

Contents

ACKNOWLEDGMENTS

We are a sum total of what we have learned from all the ones who have taught us. I am grateful for the inspiration and wisdom of the men and the women of God for what they have poured into my life.

To my loving wife, Dallas, Proverbs 18:22 says, "Whoso findeth a wife findeth a good thing, and obtaineth favor of the Lord." I thank God for hewing you out of a rock just for me in a time when marriage is fast becoming a relic of the past and commitment is falling apart. I have been blessed that our marriage has truly been made in heaven. Dallas, thank you for standing by my side; I can't imagine life without you. I love you with all my heart.

To my beautiful children, Michael, Anthony, Tchlandra, and Michelle, you are so special to me. You believed in and stood by your dad no matter what. Thank you for making me a very proud dad. I love you all. To my grandchildren who believe that their papa can do anything. I am very proud of all of you. I love you all.

To the New Birth Christian Center family, thank you for your faithfulness, prayers, and patience, which have inspired me to continue fulfilling my purpose. I love you.

To my spiritual father and mother, Maurice and Brenda Wright, thank you for the inspiration, and the impartation that you have imputed into my life. You are a blessing to the body of Christ.

To E.B Kelly, my father who begot me in the ministry and the St. Mary Baptist Church family in Lincoln, Alabama, thank you for all the years that you helped me along life's journey. Thank you Pastor Kelly and Lady Elizabeth for the guidance you have shown Dallas and me over the years. You have contributed a great deal to my success. Thank you, and I love you.

INTRODUCTION

Satan has placed highly trained and skilled taskmasters over you to afflict you with pain, low self-esteem, and a poverty mentality. This taskmaster is something or someone designed just for you to keep you in bondage in an impoverished state of mind and immobile.

You know what you want to do and what you need to do, but you can't function, because the Enemy has left you in a paralyzed state of mind. You want to move and even have the strength to move, but there is a voice inside your head that keeps talking saying the same thing to you over and over. That voice is designed to keep the cycle of bad thoughts in your head.

If you refuse to terminate the cycle and instead allow it to be passed down from generation to generation, you will keep producing stagnant, non-prospering offspring that will never progress in their spiritual walks. That's why it is so important to renew our minds with right thinking.

CHAPTER 1

Stop Limiting God

Growing up I heard many things from various people in the church world. Much of it had great value and truth, but some of it was just bad teaching. Many people taught what they thought they knew about Jesus and how we can receive from Him, rather than what the Word really says. And for years I reaped the fruits of what I'd heard as a child.

But I want to challenge you to empty your mind of the bad teaching that you grew up with—those boundary-base teachings that you received. Instead, condition your mind to look beyond just getting your needs met, to possessing nations. Let us stop limiting God! One of the saddest realities that many people face today is that they fence themselves in and then complain about the living space that they have been given. Why complain about your living space when you were the one that designed the room?

The apostle Paul wrote this to the Corinthian church:

> Dear, dear Corinthians, I can't tell you how much I long for you to enter this wide-open, spacious life. We didn't fence you in. the smallness you feel comes from within you. Your lives aren't small, but you're living them in a small way. I'm speaking as plainly as I can and with great affection. Open up your lives. Live openly and expansively. (2 Corinthians 6:11–13 MSG)

In this book I want to provoke you to stop limiting God. When the Israelites were in the wilderness, they couldn't experience all that God wanted for them, because they wouldn't take him *out of the box*, as it were.

> How oft did they provoke him in the wilderness, and grieve him in the desert! Yea, they turned back and tempted God, and limited the holy one of Israel. (Psalms 78:40–41 KJV)

Look at what the Word says: They limited the Holy One of Israel. To limit means to set up a boundary or border, to draw a line that may not be passed. So when you limit God, you draw a line that the Creator Himself shall not pass. We set these barriers up, and as powerful as God is, He will not go beyond them. I want to help you break through the natural and step into the supernatural. But this depends upon how much confidence you have in God.

> And this is the confidence that we have in
> Him that, if we ask anything according to
> his will, he heareth us: And if we know that
> he hear us, whatsoever we ask, we know we
> have the petition that we desire of Him. (1
> John 5:14–15 KJV)

The answer is not in your asking but in your confidence. Reading that passage should have caused joy to come over you. If it didn't, it could be because it had to be filtered through who you are. When you read it, you read it through *you*.

You set the boundaries in requesting anything from God. You may have been conditioned to receive only your basic needs from Him, and that limits your ability to expand what you ask God for. Jesus said in Matthew 7:2, "With the same measure you use, it will be measured back to you." So, how far do you measure the promise?

> Let me tell you what God said next. He
> said, "You're my son, and today is your
> birthday. What do you want? Name it:
> Nations as a present? Continents as a prize?
> You can command them all to dance for
> you, Or throw them out with tomorrow's
> trash. (Psalm 2:7–8 MSG)

God wants to give you the world, and you are just asking Him to meet a basic need. You are looking at a need and God is trying to give you nations. You can't think *world*, because you are trapped inside of *you*, and this limits your ability to expand what you ask for.

We tend to look at things naturally rather than in the spirit. Scriptures such as Psalm 2:7–8 must be read in the spirit. The natural man can't grab a hold of their meaning.

> But as it is written, Eye hath not seen, nor ear heard, neither have entered into the heart of man, the things which God hath prepared for them that love him.

> But God hath revealed them unto us by his spirit; for the spirit searcheth all things, yea the deep things of God. (1 Corinthians 2:9–10 KJV)

Many have a problem envisioning the world because their minds have been conditioned to receive only the basic. You will never walk in what you believe if you don't change the way you think.

Too many times, religious leaders argue that what we ask may not be granted, but that God will give us what we need, and what's best for us. In other words, God will substitute something in the place of what you have asked for. There is not a word in the Scriptures that teaches such a doctrine. Why would God say that I can have something (providing that I've met the condition of John 15:7) and then say it's not in my best interest to receive it?

Let me put it another way. You received a coupon from a local grocery exchange. It says *buy one and get one free.* You show up to redeem the offer; you buy one because that was the condition of getting the other free. You walk up to the checkout counter, but to your surprise the manager says, "I know what I've advertised, but I have come to the conclusion that getting two of these wouldn't be good for you. So, I'm limiting you to just one because you can't handle two right now. Two would make you sick!"

How will you react? You will have a fit! You will argue and debate with that manager because you know what was advertised, and furthermore, you have the proof of that advertised item in your hand. And you will refuse to be denied. Why? Because you met the condition: you bought one.

Now, if you can be that adamant and sure about a coupon in the mail from a local grocery store, what about God's Word? Of course, you must meet the condition: "If you abide in me and my words abide in you, ye shall ask what ye will and it shall be done unto you" (John 15:7 KJV).

Now, you have met the condition; you abided in Him and His Word abides in you. Why can't you ask what you will? You have the proof of God's advertised items in your hand— that is His Word.

Have you met the conditions of John 15:7? Then why are you afraid to ask?

Notes

CHAPTER 2

The Key to Answered Prayer

If you abide in me and my words abide in you, ye shall ask what ye will and it shall be done unto you. —John 15:7 KJV

Do you really understand what Jesus is saying in the quote above? If you can grab a hold of this concept, which is the message of this book, this year will be a year of abundance and answered prayer for you. But you will never walk in what you believe until you change the way you think.

Jesus said, "If ye abide in me ..." *Abide* is derived from the Greek word *meno*, which means "to remain, to dwell in continually." Dwell continually—not visit or be a guest. If you're not experiencing the abundance God has promised, perhaps you are only visiting the place where God wants you to live. God is saying to you that if you stop visiting Him and start living with Him, you can start reaping the benefits—not as a visitor, but as a resident.

Only by abiding can you enjoy the most rewarding friendship with God and experience the greatest abundance for His glory. An ongoing, vital connection with God will directly determine the amount of His power at work in your life. If you stay connected to Him, if you draw spiritual nourishment from Him, if you will allow the power that flows through Him to flow through you, nothing will be able to hold you back from living a victorious and powerful life.

Many are living beneath the place where God has purposed for them to live. Jesus said He came that we may have life and have it more abundantly. He wants you to experience life *overflowing*. When you abide in Him that carries with it a promise of answered prayer.

> If ye abide in me, and my words abide in
> you, ye shall ask what ye will, and it shall
> be done unto you. (John 15:7)

Nothing pleases God more than when we ask Him for what He wants to give us. When we abide in Him, His promise is that we can *ask what we will*. This plainly teaches that answered prayer is up to the child of God as to what he wants. Remember this passage from the Psalms:

> Let me tell you what God said next. He said,
> you're my son, and today is your birthday.

What do you want? Name it: Nations as a present?

Continents as a prize? You can command them all to dance for you,

Or throw them out with tomorrow's trash. (Psalm 2:7–8 MSG)

Those who abide in Christ, and in whom His Word abides, can get what they want as well as what they need. Both the Old and New Testaments are in agreement on that.

The Lord is my Shepherd; I shall not want. (Psalm 23:1 KJV)

O fear the LORD, ye his saints, for there is no want to them that fear Him. The young lions do lack and suffer hunger, but they that seek the Lord shall not want any good thing. (Psalm 34:9–10 KJV)

Ask and it shall be given you; seek and ye shall find; knock and it shall be opened unto you: For everyone that asketh receiveth; and he that seeketh findeth; and to him that knocketh it shall be opened. (Matthew 7:7–8 KJV)

Now unto him that is able to do exceeding abundantly above all that we ask or think, according to the power that worketh in us … (Ephesians 3:20 KJV)

Beloved, if our heart condemn us not, then have we confidence toward God. And whatsoever we ask, we receive of him, because we keep his commandments, and do those things that are pleasing in his sight. (1 John 3:21–22 KJV)

O fear the LORD, ye his saints: for *there is* no want to them that fear him. The young lions do lack, and suffer hunger: but they that seek the LORD shall not want any good *thing*. (Psalm 34:9–10 KJV)

And Jesus answering saith unto them, Have faith in God. For verily I say unto you, That whosoever shall say unto this mountain, Be thou removed, and be thou cast into the sea; and shall not doubt in his heart, but shall believe that those things which he saith shall come to pass; he shall have whatsoever he saith. Therefore I say unto you, what things soever ye desire, when ye pray, believe that ye receive *them*, and ye shall have *them*. (Mark 11: 22–24 KJV)

Whatever things you desire, when you pray, believe that you receive them, and you shall have them. If you are going to change your mind so you can walk in what you believe, then this has to stay before you and become a part of you.

When you understand that God cannot deny Himself, you can walk boldly in what He said. But remember, you cannot walk in what you believe, or live the life of abundance, until you change the way you think.

Proverbs 23:7 declares, "For as a man thinketh in his heart, so is he." Belief takes place in the spirit, but thinking takes place in the mind. It is through your will, your feelings, and your mind that Satan seeks to attack. You can believe one thing and think something totally different. What you think is what you become not what you believe. This is the reason why it is so important that you renew your mind.

> And be not conformed to this world: but
> be ye transformed by the renewing of your
> mind, that ye may prove what is that good
> and acceptable and perfect will of God.
> (Romans 12:2 KJV)

Don't let the world around you squeeze you into its way of thinking. When you come into the kingdom of God, you should abandon the thought pattern and lifestyle of the world. What do we mean when we say *world*? This refers to a society or system that man has built in order to make himself happy without God.

Don't be conformed to this world, but be transformed by the renewing of your mind. We as a people have learned how to update everything else around us:

We update our computers.

We update our clothes.

We update our vehicles.

We update our music.

We update our houses.

But many of us refuse to update our minds. We want to hold on to what we think we know rather than embrace what we don't understand, which requires change. If you change the way you think, then you can experience the direct guidance of God in your life. Paul writes "That we may know what is that good and acceptable and perfect will of God."

God is concerned about your mind. If He can get your mind out of the wilderness, He can get your body out. The problem is not what you believe, but what you think. You will never respond to what you believe if you don't change the way you think. If you change the way you think, then you can have the abundant life that you were promised. Right believing always leads to right living. You will never live right until you believe right.

If I can get you to grab hold of this concept, you will change your mind-set about what He said you can have.

Now, pray this prayer with me:

Heavenly Father, I come to You now in the name of our Lord and Savior, Jesus Christ. I bow before Thee, and I enter Your gates with thanksgiving; I enter Your courts with praise. Heavenly

Father, I ask You to forgive me of all my sins, trespasses, and iniquities. Heavenly Father, I ask You, according to Isaiah 22:22, to open the gates of heaven above me and bless me. I ask You, heavenly Father, to open the gates of favor, provision, deliverance, wisdom, protection, and healing for each of us, in Jesus' name. Father, I ask You to open those gates so that I would be blessed and that I can be in Your divine destiny. Heavenly father, I ask that I would be blessed to use these blessings in Your kingdom according to Your destiny and will for my life in the name of Jesus Christ of Nazareth, according to John 14:14. To God be the glory. Amen.

Notes

CHAPTER 3

Open My Eyes So I Can Walk in What I Believe

That the God of our Lord Jesus Christ, the Father of glory, may give unto you the spirit of wisdom and revelation in the knowledge of him: The eyes of your understanding being enlightened; that ye may know what is the hope of his calling, and what the riches of the glory of his inheritance in the saints, And what *is* the exceeding greatness of his power to us-ward who believe, according to the working of his mighty power.

—Ephesians 1:17–19 KJV

It is through these eyes that we know the hope of His calling.

The Hope of His Calling

What is involved in the calling of the Christian? Your calling involves everything that God has done, is doing, and wants to do. Paul is simply saying, "I just told you about what God has done for you. Now I want you to understand it more deeply—deeper in your heart." It involves more than being blessed with spiritual blessings and the joy of being chosen by Christ before the foundation of the world. It involves being redeemed by His blood, being adopted by God, and being sealed in Him with the Spirit.

When you begin to understand what is the hope of His calling in your life, the assurance and certainty associated with that calling, then whatever comes your way, you can stand fast on the truth of what God has accomplished for you in Christ, in the past, present, and future. Knowing these truths in a deeper, more intuitive way, will change the way you think so you can walk in what you believe. This is why Paul prayed for the eyes of their hearts to really understand these truths.

What Are the Riches of His Glory of His Inheritance in the Saints?

As saints, we are God's inheritance, His treasure, and His prize. Our riches are in God; God's riches are in His saints. When you begin to understand that you are part of a royal priesthood, it will transform your mind so you can walk in what you believe.

> But ye *are* a chosen generation, a royal priesthood, an holy nation, a peculiar people; that ye should shew forth the praises of him who hath called you out of darkness into his marvelous light ... (1 Peter 2:9 KJV)

You must understand that you are "a people of God's own possession so that you may proclaim the excellencies of Him who has called you out of darkness into His marvelous light." God considers each of us to be His precious portion. We have His seal on us, and more accurately, within us, in the presence of His Holy Spirit. Do you know why some of God's children lead lives so much fuller and richer than others? It is in the difference of their appropriations of God.

Some have learned the happy art of receiving and utilizing every inch of the knowledge of God that has been revealed to them. Simply put, their minds have been transformed so they can walk into what they believe. You cannot do that until you change the way you think. We must keep nothing back. There must be no reserve in any part of our beings. Spirit, soul, and body must be freely yielded to God.

Finally, Paul writes that we may "know the greatness of His power." What is the *greatness of the power to us who believe*? It is the power that He wrought in Christ when He raised Him from the dead. That resurrection power is what works in every believer. The power that raised Christ is working in you! If you can get this in your spirit, then you can walk in divine authority.

> Verily, verily, I say unto you, He that
> believeth on me, the works that I do shall he
> do also; and greater *works* than these shall
> he do; because I go unto my Father. (John
> 14:12 KJV)

What I can do is related to where I came from. That means that my ability is defined by God's ability. Everything in life gets its potential from where it was taken from. The plant's potential to grow healthy abides in the potential of the soil. The fish has to stay in the water to live and reproduce. God said that we were made in His likeness and image (Genesis 1:26–28). If you want to know what you can do, find out what God can do. If you want to know your ability, look at God's ability. If you are going to walk in power and authority, then you must know who you are in Christ.

God wants you to realize all that He has prepared for you, so the third item in Paul's prayer for his converts is that they might know the exceeding greatness of His power toward us who believe. It's power! It's *His* power! It's *great* power; nothing less would suffice. It is *exceeding* great power, beyond our comprehension. Yes, *the eyes of our understanding being enlightened* refers to an inner awareness provided by the Holy Spirit, enabling us to realize everything that God has made available to us.

If you can ever get your inner man enlightened, or have a light to come on inside you so that you know what belongs to you, then you will start walking in power. When you know what belongs to you, you'll stop falling to pieces over small things. Maybe your spirit hadn't been trained for big things yet. You have trained it for small things but not big things. Many have trained their minds to only getting their basic needs met when God wants to give us nations. This takes you to a place where your mind hasn't been trained to go. These are the deep things of God.

> But as it is written, Eye hath not seen, nor ear heard, neither have entered into the heart of man, the things which God hath prepared for them that love him But God hath revealed *them* unto us by his Spirit: for the Spirit searcheth all things, yea, the deep things of God. (1 Corinthians 2:9–10 KJV)

Notice that He searches *all* things. And while He is looking at everything, He pulls up the deep things. Our spirits go on a hunt, or search, for deep things. God takes us in the spirit where we can never go in the flesh. Some people's minds are still shallow because their spirits haven't been trained for deep things. This is the reason why many can't comprehend what Jesus said in Mark 11:22–24.

And Jesus answering saith unto them, Have faith in God. For verily I say unto you, That whosoever shall say unto this mountain, Be thou removed, and be thou cast into the sea; and shall not doubt in his heart, but shall believe that those things which he saith shall come to pass; he shall have whatsoever he saith. Therefore I say unto you, what things so ever ye desire, when ye pray, believe that ye receive *them*, and ye shall have *them*.

Many haven't received this revelation yet.

Jesus said, "What things you desire when you pray, believe that you receive them and you shall have them." That disqualifies a lot of people because they don't desire anything, or if they do, they talk in a contradictory way. They say they want it but are always talking negative about getting it.

> If any man among you seem to be religious,
> and bridleth not his tongue, but deceiveth
> his own heart, this man's religion is vain.

> (James 1:26 KJV)

How can anyone deceive his or her own heart? When you speak out of your mouth what you really don't want, your heart doesn't know that you don't want it, so it goes to work to produce what you said you wanted. Your heart is a production center; it goes to work to produce what you've said. So you deceive your heart. Remember, Proverbs 18:21 states that life and death are in the power of the tongue. Every person is judged by his words because they reveal the state of the heart. Your mouth reveals where your heart has been living.

> Of the abundance of the heart his mouth
> speaketh. (Luke 6:45 KJV)

Many saints of God don't experience answered prayer, because of heart issues. If you can get your heart and mouth in agreement, then you can have what you say. Stop planting the seed of doubt and cursing the very soil that your seed is sown in. The seed that isn't sown on properly prepared soil and cared for will fail to bring forth fruit.

> And he spake many things unto them in parables, saying, Behold, a sower went forth to sow; And when he sowed, some *seeds* fell by the way side, and the fowls came and devoured them up: Some fell upon stony places, where they had not much earth: and forthwith they sprung up, because they had no deepness of earth: And when the sun was up, they were scorched; and because they had no root, they withered away. And some fell among thorns; and the thorns sprung up, and choked them: (Matthew 13:3–7 KJV)

Words are like seeds. They have the ability to create in you what you say about yourself. In a story recounted in the book of Numbers, ten of the twelve spies saw themselves as grasshoppers.

> But the men that went up with him said, We be not able to go up against the people; for they are stronger than we. And they brought up an evil report of the land which they had searched unto the children of Israel, saying, the land, through which we have gone to search it, is a land that eateth up the inhabitants thereof; and all the people that we saw in it *are* men of a great stature. And there we saw the giants, the

> sons of Anak, *which come* of the giants: and
> we were in our own sight as grasshoppers,
> and so we were in their sight. (Numbers
> 13:31–33 KJV)

The giants never saw them as grasshoppers; they saw themselves as grasshoppers. You will never walk in what you believe until you change what you are saying about yourself.

> For by thy words thou shalt be justified,
> and by thy words thou shalt be condemned.
> (Matthew 13:37 KJV)

Learn how to discipline your flesh when it is under pressure to say only what God says. Everything else is a lie. The key to victory in your life is in your mouth. It is tied up in what you are saying about yourself. And what you are saying about yourself is how you really see yourself. The way you see yourself shapes your destiny. You can either speak life to yourself, or you can speak death. Be careful of the words you speak and the words you take heed to because they have creative ability. When you grab hold of these truths, things will begin to change.

Notes

CHAPTER 4

Changing the Way I Think

My little children, of whom I travail in
birth again until Christ be formed in you.

Galatians 4:19 KJV

The book of Galatians derives its title (*Pros Galatas*) from
the region in Asia Minor (modern-day Turkey) where
the church was located. Paul wrote the book to counter
Judaizing false teachers who were undermining the central
New Testament doctrine of justification by faith. These false
teachers were spreading false information that the Gentiles
must first become Jewish proselytes and submit to all the
Mosaic Law before they could become Christians.

Paul, shocked by the Galatians' openness to receive such
teaching, wrote this letter to defend justification by faith
and to warn the churches of the consequences of abandoning

this essential doctrine. In chapter four he argues from the standpoint of an heir receiving an inheritance.

> Now I say, *that* the heir, as long as he is
> a child, differeth nothing from a servant,
> though he be lord of all; (Galatians 4:1 KJV)

Heir refers to a child too young to talk; a minor, spiritually and intellectually immature, not ready for the privileges and responsibility of adulthood. As long as you are a child, God can't give you what He would give to someone mature. Your abundance can be hindered because your level of maturity is not where it should be. So, God can't give you what He wants to until you mature. Therefore you will remain under a tutor until you grow up. You have the right to abundance because you are an heir, but because you are still under a tutor, you can't get it. The moment you are released from your tutorial, God can release your inheritance. If He releases it to you while you are still immature, you will waste it because your mind has not been conditioned to receive it.

Paul had so much compassion for the Galatians because he wanted them to receive everything that Christ had for them. He writes, "My little children, of whom I travail in birth again until Christ be formed in you" (Galatians 4:19 KJV).

This is so interesting! He calls them *little children*, as though he is a parent responsible for their well-being. He talks in a language that says *with everything that is going on around you and in the church, I am responsible for your spiritual growth.* He is saying, in essence, *It is my duty to disciple you, to make* sure that this type of false teaching and false doctrine doesn't get in you so you can experience the abundant life.

He says, "My little children, for whom I labor in birth again until Christ is *formed* in you" (emphasis added). According to the English Dictionary, the word *form* refers to "the shape and structure of an object. The mode in which a thing exists, acts, or manifests itself. "Behavior according to a fixed or accepted standard."

I want Christ to be formed in you—to manifest Himself in you, so you can:

Act like Him.

Behave like Him.

And, so His standards will become your standards.

It is my responsibility to teach that carnal nature out of you so that Christ can be formed in you, so you can walk in what you believe and reach that next level of abundance. You can never change the way you think, and walk in what you believe, until Christ has been formed in you.

How do I know when Christ is formed in me?

I have a love for the brethren.

> A new commandment I give unto you, that ye love one another; as I have loved you, that ye also love one another. By this shall

> all *men* know that ye are my disciples, if
> ye have love one to another. (John 13:34–
> 35 KJV).

> Beloved, let us love one another: for love is
> of God; and every one that loveth is born of
> God, and knoweth God. (1 John 4:7 KJV)

> We know that we have passed from death
> unto life, because we love the brethren. He
> that loveth not *his* brother abideth in death.
> (1 John 3:14 KJV)

God is not talking about superficial love. We as a people use this word *love* too loosely today. And the very thing that we say we love today we hate tomorrow. The very person we say we love today and laid down with last night we are ready to walk away from the next day. Our love should reach beyond what we see and who a person is and love them in spite of.

How do I know when Christ is fully formed in me? When I can trust wholly in Him.

> And Caleb stilled the people before Moses,
> and said let us go up at once, and possesses
> it; for we are well able to overcome it.
> (Numbers 13:30 KJV)

Kadesh-Barnea was a place of decision for Israel. It involved more than just taking the land that God had promised them. They had to decide whether they would follow and trust God or their own wisdom and understanding. Joshua and Caleb, looking through the eyes of faith, saw no reason to delay. They wanted to go up at once and take the land.

Now, you must understand that both reports were true. There *were* giants in the land, and yes, their walls *were* high and fortified. But two men by faith trusted God and based their trust on His promise and saw the land as theirs. Ten men trusted in themselves and knew they could not defeat the giants. Two men saw God as their deliverer while the other ten believed that man must deliver himself. Two men were willing to let God use them. Ten men opposed God's will and hindered others.

But Joshua and Caleb wholly trusted God!

> Trust in the LORD with all thine heart; and lean not unto thine own understanding. In all thy ways acknowledge Him and he shall direct thy paths. (Proverbs 3:5–6 KJV)

Caleb, still claiming God's blessing, cries, "Give me this mountain" (Joshua 14:12). Hebron became Caleb's inheritance because he wholly followed God (Joshua 14:14).

You must understand that Caleb's circumstances were no different from those of any of the other Israelites. Yet he was a man who believed God and trusted Him. He let God save him and direct his path. Do you wholly trust Him today?

How do I know when Christ is fully formed in me? I obey His teachings.

> Jesus answered and said unto him, If a man love me, he will keep my words: and my Father will love him, and we will come unto him, and make our abode with him.
>
> He that loveth me not keepeth not my sayings; and the word which ye hear is not mine, but the Father's which sent me. (John 14:23–24 KJV).

The instructions you follow today will determine the future you create tomorrow.

> Make thee an ark of gopher wood; rooms shalt thou make in the ark, and shalt pitch it within and without with pitch. And this is the fashion which thou shalt make it *of*:
>
> The length of the ark *shall be* three hundred cubits, the breadth of it fifty cubits, and the height of it thirty cubits. A window shalt thou make to the ark, and in a cubit shalt thou finish it above; and the door of the ark shalt thou set in the side thereof; *with* lower, second, and third *stories* shalt thou make it. (Genesis 6:14–16 KJV)

God gave Noah specific instruction on how to build the ark. Noah built the ark exactly the way he was instructed. The instructions you follow today will determine the future you create.

> And it came to pass after these things that
> God did tempt Abraham, and said unto
> him, Abraham: and he said, Behold, here I
> am. And he said, Take now thy son, thine
> only son Isaac, whom thou lovest, and get
> thee into the land of Moriah; and offer him
> there for a burnt offering upon one of the
> mountains which I will tell thee of. And
> Abraham rose up early in the morning, and
> saddled his ass, and took two of his young
> men with him, and Isaac his son, and clave
> the wood for the burnt offering, and rose
> up, and went unto the place of which God
> had told him. (Gen 22:1-3 KJV)

This is the type of obedience God will respond to!

God doesn't give you stuff he gives you and instruction; then based on how well you follow the instructions that he has given you that you get the stuff. He gave Abraham an instruction, and when Abraham obeyed the instruction, he received the blessing. Don't overlook the instructions in trying to get the stuff.

God gave Noah an instruction to save his family: *build an ark*. If he hadn't built the ark, he and his family would have perished.

Instructions! He gave the widow who approached the prophet Elisha an instruction.

Then he said, Go, borrow thee vessels abroad of all thy neighbours, *even* empty vessels; borrow not a few. And when thou art come in, thou shalt shut the door upon thee and upon thy sons, and shalt pour out into all those vessels, and thou shalt set aside that which is full. So she went from him, and shut the door upon her and upon her sons, who brought *the vessels* to her; and she poured out. And it came to pass, when the vessels were full, that she said unto her son, Bring me yet a vessel. And he said unto her,

There is not a vessel more. And the oil stayed. Then she came and told the man of God. And he said, Go, sell the oil, and pay thy debt, and live thou and thy children of the rest. (2 Kings: 4:3–7 KJV)

Now, pray this prayer with me:

Father, in the name of Jesus I bind my mind to the will of God. Lord, it is not my will to be conformed to this world but to be transformed by the renewing of my mind that I may prove good, acceptable, and perfect to what Your will is. Teach me to abhor what is evil and cling to what is good. Thank You, Lord, for a renewed mind! In Jesus' name. Amen.

Notes

CHAPTER 5

You Cannot Conquer What You Are Not Willing to Face

You cannot possess what you have been promised until you leave where you are. You have been in this place long enough. If you leave it, He will take you to the promise. The land that God is taking you into is nothing like the place that you just left. There, the Enemy abused you, walked over you, ridiculed you, and held you in captivity. The place where God is about to take you is going to be better. Rather than the Enemy having his foot on your neck, you will have *your* foot on *his* neck.

> Every place that the sole of your foot shall tread upon, that I have given unto you, as I said unto Moses. (Joshua 1:3 KJV)

God tells Joshua that the place was not going to come to him; he must go to the place. Could it be that you haven't occupied your place yet because you haven't put your foot on it? You cannot tread upon anything that you are not willing to walk into. You will never conquer anything that you keep avoiding. The reason why many are still walking around their mountains is because they keep avoiding issues that they should be facing. You cannot conquer what you won't face. The place that God has given you is in the middle of conflict. That means that you are not going to get it without a fight. But if you are ready to contend for it, God has already given it to you. Every place that the sole of your foot shall tread upon is already yours. But your promise is in the middle of a conflict.

> From the wilderness and this Lebanon even unto the great river, the river Euphrates, all the land of the Hittites, and unto the great sea toward the going down of the sun, shall be your coast. (Joshua 1:4 KJV)

The Hittites were a great, warlike people that occupied the mountains of south Canaan. If the Israelites wanted the land, they had to go through the process. Everything is not going to come to you easy. There are some things that you will have to fight for. You may be hoping to conquer without having to go to war.

> And from the days of John the Baptist until now the kingdom of heaven suffereth violence, and the violent take it by force. (Matthew 11:12 KJV)

Many want to embrace the promise but avoid the process. You can't get the promise without going through the process. When you leave where you are to go to the promise, you must understand that there is a process. The good news is that God is going to defeat the people that stand in the way of where He's taking you. But you will not be able to conquer what you are not willing to face.

Israel couldn't conquer Canaan, because they couldn't conquer their fears. They were standing at the door of the promise but spent forty years in the wilderness because they could not conquer their fears. They saw themselves as grasshoppers when they compared themselves to the giants. God said that they were conquerors, but they said that they were grasshoppers.

And these people that should have been conquerors became wanderers because they allowed their mouths to curse their promise. Don't allow your mouth to curse your promise and cancel out where you are going.

> Because all those men which have seen
> my glory, and my miracles, which I did
> in Egypt and in the wilderness, and have
> tempted me now these ten times, and have
> nothearkened to my voice; surely they
> shall not see the land which I sware unto
> their fathers, neither shall any of them that
> provoked me see it: but my servant Caleb,
> because he had another spirit with him, and
> hath followed me fully, him will I bring
> into the land whereinto he went; and his

seed shall possess it. (Now the Amalekites and the Canaanites dwelt in the valley.) Tomorrow turn you, and get you into the wilderness by the way of the Red sea. And the LORD spake unto Moses and unto Aaron, saying, How long *shall I bear with* this evil congregation, which murmur against me? I have heard the murmurings of the children of Israel, which they murmur against me. Say unto them, *As truly as* I live, saith the LORD, as ye have spoken in mine ears, so will I do to you: your carcasses shall fall in this wilderness, and all that were numbered of you, according to your whole number, from twenty years old and upward, which have murmured against me, doubtless ye shall not come into the land, *concerning* which I sware to make you dwell therein, save Caleb the son of Jephunneh, and Joshua the son of Nun. But your little ones, which ye said should be a prey, them will I bring in, and they shall know the land which ye have despised But as for you, your carcasses, they shall fall in this wilderness. And your children shall wander in the wilderness forty years, and bear your whoredoms, until your carcasses be wasted in the wilderness. After the number of the days in which ye searched the land, *even* forty days, each day for a year, shall ye bear your iniquities, *even* forty years,

and ye shall know my breach of promise.
(Numbers 14:22–34 KJV)

Some wander for years in a place that they are bigger than because they failed to face the very thing that they fear. Fear will cripple you and cause you to make bad choices. Fear will cause you to procrastinate when you should be moving. Fear has torment in it. Telling someone that *they have nothing to fear but fear itself* is good rhetoric but bad medicine because fear itself is a deadly enemy that can destroy you.

Fear can distort reality and deaden you to common sense. You will not be able to see things as they are, because you will be looking at them through the eyes of fear. Either we learn how to control our fears or our fears will end up controlling us—and destroying us. Either you face your fears and fix them or they will fix you. When you are trying to overcome fear, you are engaged in warfare. And you must understand that one battle will not win the war. You've got to keep fighting on your knees until you feel the fear release its hold and go back to wherever it came from.

God hath not given us the spirit of fear; but
of power, and of love, and of a sound mind.
(2 Timothy 1:7 KJV)

Now, pray this prayer with me:

Heavenly Father, I thank You that it is written: "For the weapons of our warfare are not carnal, but mighty through God to pulling down strong holds; Casting down imaginations, and every high thing that exalteth itself against the knowledge of

God, and bring into captivity every thought to the obedience of Christ," according to 2 Corinthians 10:4–5. Heavenly Father, I pull down every demonic stronghold, doubt, confusion, and fear that I have in my mind today. I pull them down and cast them aside in the name of our Lord, Jesus Christ. I pull down every vain imagination in me. I pull them down and cast them aside in Jesus' name. I pull down every high thought in me that exalts itself against the knowledge of God. I pull them down and cast them aside in Jesus' name. I ask You now to cause Your anointing to destroy any yokes of bondage, including fear, doubt, lust, or drugs, along with all their works, roots, fruits, and links that are in my life. In Jesus' name. Amen.

Notes

49

CHAPTER 6

Conquering the Giants That Are Keeping Me From My Promise

Hear, O Israel: Thou art to pass over Jordan this day, to go in to possess nations greater and mightier than thyself, cities great and fenced up to heaven, people great and tall, the children of the An'akim, whom thou knowest, and of whom thou hast heard say, Who can stand before the children of Anak! Understand therefore this day, that the LORD thy God is he which goeth over before thee; as a consuming fire he shall destroy them, and he shall bring them down before thy face: so shalt thou drive

them out, and destroy them quickly, as the
LORD hath said unto thee.

—Deuteronomy 9:1–3 KJV

Life is full of ups and downs, tests and trials. Some tests and
trials bring us to a standstill. They seem to impose a wall
that we cannot climb. We find ourselves sitting beneath
that wall wondering what to do next. If you have come to
the end of your rope, a wall that you cannot scale, or giants
that you cannot conquer, I've got news for you. We serve a
risen Savior that will bring us through every trial and test
and slay every giant that is standing in our way! One of the
reasons for what you are experiencing is that God is testing
you to see what you are made of.

> And thou shalt remember all the way which
> the LORD thy God led thee these forty
> years in the wilderness, to humble thee,
> and to prove thee, to know what was in
> thine heart, whether thou wouldest keep
> his commandments, or no. (Deuteronomy
> 8:2 KJV)

The Message Bible says it like this:

> Remember every road that God led you on
> for forty years in the wilderness, pushing
> you to your limits, testing you so that he
> would know what you are made of, whether
> you will keep his commandment or not.
> (Deuteronomy 8:2 MSG)

He took you through this stage in your life so you would know that "man cannot live by bread alone, but by every word that comes from the mouth of God. There are those that think that they can live by their possessions alone. They love to take pride in living on what they have as though that is all they need." You cannot live by your own possessions alone. Neither can you depend upon the world system for if you do, it will produce worry and doubt. Possessions alone will not satisfy. You may have His hand, but without His face you are still empty.

> When thou saidest seek my face, my heart
> said unto thee, thy face, Lord, will I seek.
>
> (Psalm 27:8 KJV)

You can never make it in this life by obtaining physical things alone; you need His Word. Where God is about to take you, you won't be able to depend on your natural resources. You must understand that there is a supernatural presence at work as well. He will be taking you through a season like no other you have ever gone through so that you will understand He is your provider.

As He says to the Israelites about to enter the Promised Land,

> Hear, O Israel: Thou art to pass over Jordan
> this day, to go in to possess nations greater
> and mightier than thyself, cities great and
> fenced up to heaven, people great and tall,
> the children of the An'akim, whom thou

knowest, and of whom thou hast heard say, Who can stand before the children of Anak! Understand therefore this day, that the LORD thy God is he which goeth over before thee; as a consuming fire he shall destroy them, and he shall bring them down before thy face: so shalt thou drive them out, and destroy them quickly, as the LORD hath said unto thee. (Deuteronomy 9:1–3 KJV)

The giants you will face are large—too big for you to handle alone.

Job cut back. Giant!

Job layoff. Giant!

Foreclosure. Giant!

Sickness. Giant!

Addiction. Giant!

Financial problems. Giant!

These giants are strong, and they have the potential to destroy you or keep you from getting your breakthrough. But have I got news for you! You don't have to be intimidated by them. God—your God—is with you; God majestic, God awesome. He will move them out of your way and fight for you. Good news! These giants are going to fall!

They have been holding up your blessings for too long.

You have cried for too many nights because of them.

You have lost too many things because of them.

You have missed too many blessings because they stood in your way.

> Understand therefore this day, that the LORD thy God is he which goeth over before thee; as a consuming fire he shall destroy them, and he shall bring them down before thy face: so shalt thou drive them out, and destroy them quickly, as the LORD hath said unto thee. (Deuteronomy 9:3 KJV)

God is bringing them *down* so they can't stop you anymore.

Down so they won't keep you up all night!

Down so you will no longer be depressed all the time!

These giants are about to fall so you might as well get ready for a takeover!

Are You Ready for a Takeover?

You are about to walk into a new dimension, into a place where you have never been before.

> Hear, O Israel: Thou *art* to pass over Jordan
> this day, to go in to possess nations greater
> and mightier than thyself, cities great and
> fenced up to heaven ... (Deuteronomy
> 9:1 KJV)

When are they to pass over Jordan? *This day!* You are going to pass over this day and possess those things that were unattainable. The walls that were built to keep you out will come down.

Walls are nothing new for us as a people. We have been struggling with walls all of our lives.

I am not worried about the walls.

I am not going to fall to pieces over the walls.

I am not going to stress out about the walls. Why?

The walls that have been built to keep me out are coming down!

The giants that have been ruling your life—that stood tall and influenced you to make bad decisions, that said you couldn't defeat them—are about to fall! God is going before you to bring them down before your eyes.

The reason the Devil is oppressing you and trying to keep you out is because it is a good land.

> For the LORD thy God bringeth thee into a good land, a land of brooks of water, of fountains and depths that spring out of valleys and hills; a land of wheat, and barley, and vines, and fig trees, and pomegranates; a land of olive oil, and honey; a land wherein thou shalt eat bread without scarceness, thou shalt not lack any thing in it; a land whose stones are iron, and out of whose hills thou mayest dig brass. (Deuteronomy 8:7–9 KJV)

It is a good land, a place of no lack. The only thing that will keep you from prospering in this new place is disobedience and not responding in faith.

God will never take you beyond your last act of disobedience. When He has told you to do something and you refused, God will not move you beyond that point. What has God told you to do that you haven't done it yet? You could be right at the door of the promise and yet not enter in because of your last act of disobedience.

Don't allow your promise to be held up because of these giants of disobedience, fear, doubt, and anxiety. You are bigger than these things that are trying to hinder your breakthrough.

Read on!

Notes

CHAPTER 7

You Are Stronger Than Those Things That Are Holding You Down

The book of Exodus derives its name from a word meaning "exit" or "departure." God wants to bring you out of whatever has you bound. In Hebrew, the book begins with the conjunction *and,* emphasizing that it was thought of as a continuation of Genesis. Exodus opens where Genesis leaves off: with Jacob's descendants multiplying in Egypt. A new ruler emerges who respects neither the memory of Jacob nor the rights of the Israelites. So they go from freedom to slavery.

All Pharaoh can see is a people prospering and growing, and this becomes a threat to him. Your prosperity and growth are a direct threat to the enemy. He knows that if you continue to prosper and grow spiritually, he can't hold you in bondage any longer.

In chapter 1 Pharaoh makes a statement that raises a question.

> And he said unto his people, Behold, the people of the children of Israel are more and mightier than we. (Exodus 1:9 KJV)

The question is: If I am bigger and stronger than you, how can you hold me down? You would have to change the way I think, and keep afflicting me with oppression and depression.

In this same way, if you are not careful, your enemies will devise a plan to hold you in captivity.

> Come on, let us deal wisely with them; lest they multiply, and it come to pass, that, when there falleth out any war, they join also unto our enemies, and fight against us, and so get them up out of the land. Therefore they did set over them taskmasters to afflict them with their burdens. And they built for Pharaoh treasure cities, Pithom and Raam'ses. But the more they afflicted them, the more they multiplied and grew. And they were grieved because of the children of Israel. And the Egyptians made the children of Israel to serve with rigor: and they made their lives bitter with hard

> bondage, in mortar, and in brick, and in
> all manner of service in the field: all their
> service, wherein they made them serve, was
> with rigor. (Deuteronomy 1:1–14 KJV)

The Enemy will devise a plan to break your morale, to wear you down under heavy loads in order to mess up your thinking. For example, he has devised a plan to remove our men from their children's lives. When the man is removed from the home or is not present in the home that home becomes what God never designed it to be; an incomplete family. And because of this, Gallup has some sobering statistics about the moral condition of America: *Every second* a child is suspended from school; *every seventy seconds* a child is arrested; *every two hours* (or less) a child under twenty is shot to death on the streets; *every four hours* a child under twenty dies by his own hand.

Gallup reports that the number of students between the ages of twelve and eighteen who are involved in some form of prostitution to support their drug addiction could fill the Rose Bowl, the Cotton Bowl, the Sugar Bowl, the Orange Bowl, and the Fiesta Bowl.

Forty percent of America's fourteen-year-old girls will become pregnant before their nineteenth birthdays.

Almost 60 percent of evangelical Christian students ages twelve through eighteen are sexually active.

Child abuse in America is up 200 percent since 1976.

The number of sexually abused children is up 1075 percent since 1962.

Who do you think these children are? They are the children of parents that are held captive by spiritual taskmasters.

Satan has placed highly trained and skilled taskmasters over you to afflict you with pain, low self-esteem, and a poverty mentality. A taskmaster is something or someone designed just for you to keep you in bondage and in an impoverished state of mind. What the Enemy wants to do is to keep you in an immobile state.

You know what you want to do and what you need to do, but you can't function because the Enemy has left you in a paralyzed state of mind. And even though you want to move and have the strength to move, there is a voice inside your head that keeps saying the same thing over and over again. That voice is designed to keep the cycle of bad thoughts in your head.

Terminating the Cycle of Thoughts

When we speak of our thought lives, we are entering another atmosphere. Each thought has a cycle—a beginning and an end. The cycle can be renewed or terminated. If you don't terminate the cycle, it will finish what it has set out to do, and you will repeat again and again the thing that you were thinking about. Therefore it's important to practice this scriptural admonition:

> Casting down imaginations, and every high thing that exalteth itself against the knowledge of God, and bringing into captivity every thought to the obedience of Christ.

> (2 Corinthians 10:5 KJV)

If we refuse to terminate the cycle and allow it to be passed down from generation to generation, we will keep producing stagnant, non-prospering offspring that will never progress in their spiritual walks. That's why it is so important to renew our minds with right thinking:

> And be not conformed to this world: but be ye transformed by the renewing of your mind, that ye may prove what is that good, and acceptable, and perfect will of God.

> (Romans 12:2 KJV)

But when your mind is not renewed, you will repeat the cycle that has characterized your life. It may be in a different place with different people, but the experience will be the same.

You leave one job and go into another one—and repeat the same cycle.

You leave one relationship and go into another one—and repeat the same cycle.

You come out of one church and go into another one—and repeat the same cycle.

> When you repeat the same thing over and over again, it means there is no change in your life.

You are conformed to a cycle of bad thoughts, which can pull you away from your destiny and cause you to miss a season in your life. A life-changing thought begins with a suggestion. The Devil, or a human, will drop a seed in your head through a suggestion. Someone will come to you and say, "You stay in church too much," or "You're practicing too much discipleship … too much prayer … too much praising." Or, "I don't know how you've put up with that man (or that woman) this long. If I were you I would leave."

Yes, they will use the power of suggestion to pull you off course.

A thought is an unspoken word. A word has to be spoken to produce fear. That thought may be spoken by the Devil, or he might use somebody else. Now, the development of that thought depends on you; you can either receive it or reject it.

Your thought is just an unspoken word that has not been allowed access into the atmosphere of your life yet. But when you speak what you have been thinking, you open the door and give your thoughts access into your life. It is the thought life that creates the environment that you chose to live in. The atmosphere that you create defines the boundaries that you choose to live within.

Any thought left to roam will establish a mind-set that will set up a stronghold in your life. We have to pull down strongholds and bring into captivity every thought to the obedience of God. What are you sowing into your spirit all day?

> Be not deceived; God is not mocked: for whatsoever a man soweth, that shall he also reap. For he that soweth to his flesh shall of the flesh reap corruption; but he that soweth to the Spirit shall of the Spirit reap life everlasting. (Galatians 6:7–8 KJV)

My question to you again: what are you sowing into your spirit all day? What are you listening to? What do you allow to enter into your head? You cannot listen to anything and everything all day and still live a victorious life. What are you feeding your spirit? Create an atmosphere for God to dwell in. Many won't go to church or Bible study, and won't read their Word. Instead, they fill their spirits with entertainment—and then, wonder why they are defeated.

When you allow your thoughts to roam freely, they will produce other things as well.

> For from within, out of the heart of men, proceed evil thoughts, adulteries, fornications, murders, thefts, covetousness, wickedness, deceit, lasciviousness, an evil eye, blasphemy, pride, foolishness all these evil things come from within, and defile the man.

(Mark 7:21–23 KJV)

All these things begin with a thought that you have allowed to enter the atmosphere of your life.

> The theater of your mind is where the previews are shown before the show comes on.

Your thoughts are the previews that are played just before the show comes on. The ensuing action is what destroys a home, a marriage, a life, a child, a business, an individual, a church ...

Previews are what pull you into the movies. But you must understand that previews can be deceiving.

It is time to break those cycles of thoughts before they are allowed to destroy another generation. So how do you terminate these cycles of thoughts?

> Finally, brethren, whatsoever things are true, whatsoever things are honest,
>
> Whatsoever things are just, whatsoever things are pure, whatsoever things are lovely, whatsoever things are of good report; if there be an virtue, and if there be any praise, think on these things.(Philippians 4:8 KJV)

Let your mind be filled with the things of God. Create an atmosphere where your thoughts are the thoughts of God—an atmosphere for success where every thought is brought under the obedience of Christ. Whatever controls your mind controls you. If fear controls the mind, then fear will control you. If jealousy controls your mind, then jealousy will control you.

If you win the battle of the mind, you will set yourself up for a victorious life in every area. It is liberation time! It's time to leave that place of bondage. Get up from where you are and move into your wealthy place! Press on to the high calling that is yours in Christ Jesus.

Pray this prayer:

Heavenly Father, I come to You in the name of my Lord and Savior, Jesus Christ. I am standing on the truth of Your Word. You said that You would give me the keys to the kingdom, that whatever I bound on earth would be bound in heaven, and whatever I loosed on earth would be loosed in heaven, according to Matthew 16:18. Right now, in the name of Jesus I bind my will to the will of God that I may be constantly aware of Your will and purpose for my life. I bind myself to the truth of God that I will not be deceived by the lies of the world and the Devil. I do not want to react out of my own human thoughts when situations arise suddenly. Lord, I bind my feet to the path of righteousness that my steps would be steady and true all day long. I bind the strong man that I may take back every bit of joy, peace, blessing, and freedom that he has stolen from me. I take them back right now! I repent of every wrong desire, attitude, and pattern of thinking I have had. Forgive me for holding on to wrong ideals, desires, behaviors, and habits, according to 1 John 1:19 and John 14:14. I loose every wrong attitude, pattern of thinking, belief, ideal, behavior, and habit I have ever learned. I loose every wrong thought and evil imagination that would keep me from being in sweet unity with You. In Jesus' name. Amen.

Notes

You can contact Bishop Michael Truss at:

Bishopmtruss@att.net

or write to:

Mike Truss Ministry
3237 Gunnels Lane
Oxford, Al 36203